SHORT AND SWEET

also by Simon Armitage

SHORT AND SWEET
101 Very Short Poems

Edited
with an introduction by
SIMON ARMITAGE

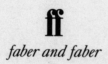

faber and faber

First published in 1999
by Faber and Faber Limited
3 Queen Square London WC1N 3AU
This edition first published in 2002

Photoset by Wilmaset Ltd, Wirral
Printed in England by Bookmarque Ltd, Croydon

A CIP record for this book
is available from the British Library
ISBN 0-571-21556-4

2 4 6 8 10 9 7 5 3 1

CONTENTS

INTRODUCTION Precious Little

I've been interested in short poems from an early age, ever since I read an entry in the *Guinness Book of Records* stating that the world's smallest poem was a piece called 'Fleas'. Here it is in its entirety:

> Adam
> 'ad 'em.

My first instinct was to try and come up with something even shorter, but after puzzling over it for a while, I decided to leave the world record intact. It's not that 'Fleas' uses the least number of letters possible – on that count it could certainly be beaten. But as a poem it manages to do so much in such a small area of space and such a short amount of time. 'Fleas', a couplet with a traditional metrical pattern, contains an internal rhyme, a concluding end-rhyme, and happens to be witty as well as making a telling observation about the nature of humankind from its mythological beginnings. Not bad for a handful of syllables. Milton could have saved himself the bother, if only he'd thought of it first.

I've been making a mental note of other short poems for a long time now, and editing this anthology gives me a chance of bringing some of them together, as well as the opportunity to say something about the type of work which otherwise keeps itself to itself.

We live in an age where we are bombarded with stuff and nonsense coming at us from every angle, most of it in the form of language. Look around, listen up: billboards, branding, signposts, satellite TV, digital radio, telecommunication, the Web, the Net, e-mail, flyers, posters, slogans, strap-lines, skywriting, newspapers, magazines, fanzines, makers' names, subscriptions, junk-mail, free offers for the making of fortunes, fridge magnets for the making of poems ... even books. Most of it is unsolicited, unavoidable, and garbage. I don't want to come the old soldier, but wasn't there a time when words were a valuable commodity, chosen carefully and painstakingly reproduced, and didn't that mean a certain amount of thought went into what people said, and where they said it? I'm not in praise of a world where loose talk costs lives, a world where a word in the wrong ear can lead a person along the plank or onto the gallows – God knows there's still enough of that kind of thing going on. But there's a difference between freedom of speech and sounding off for the sake of it. Between the right to reply and loving the sound of your own voice. Between telling it as it is and the need to fill every available inch of space and every curve in the airwaves with a noise from the throat or a letter from the alphabet.

The best literature, I feel, is a kind of written-down talk. Not talk as it might come out from between the teeth, but a sort of imagined talk. And poetry, I'd say, is a more stylized and considered version of the same thing – how conversation or monologue or even mumbling might sound if we thought about it for long enough.

Like all art forms, poetry has been affected by the era of information overload. Whether it has suffered, nobody can really say, least of all those of us who are up to our elbows in it. Poetry has always responded to and been determined by the atmosphere in which it exists, and in these highly oxygenated times, poetry seems more relevant than ever, and more effective. It has been described as 'the art form of the recession'; whether 'recession' refers to a state of economic slow-down or a general receding of intellectual integrity isn't stated. But clearly the purity of poetry and the way it can be achieved with nothing more than paper and pen are both factors in determining its contemporary importance. Poetry is one voice declaring its state of mind; it requires no back-beat, no accompaniment, no video presentation, and its construction needs no studio, no expensive materials, no police cordon and canteen wagon, and no team, committee or corporation to come up with a compromise solution.

In the past too, poetry was validated by the setting in which it appeared. In the early days, literacy was as valuable as gold or saffron, and since the advent of the printing press, it is as if one of the functions of poetry has been to act as a kind of reprimand to the increasing verbosity and long-windedness of each subsequent century.

If this all sounds like a justification for poetry in general, then a defense of the short poem extends out of the same logic. In days gone by, short poems might have been the ones that were more easily remembered, and therefore more successful. Today, it is still the short poem that stays in the mind as language, whereas longer poems tend to be remembered for their overall structure or patterning, or for the occasional quote. Robert Graves, in his essay 'Sweeney Among the Blackbirds', flirts with the argument that the long poem is nothing more than a poet's attempt at greatness, at becoming 'major'. Perhaps he has a point. On the other hand, we should be wary of the rapid-fire, magazine mentality which credits us with the attention span of a newborn baby and addresses us as customers and punters rather than readers or thinkers.

And yet the short poem, at its best, brings about an almost instantaneous surge of both understanding and sensation unavailable elsewhere; its effect should not be underestimated and its design not confused with convenience.

Poetry has sometimes been described in visual terms, in as much as a short poem might resemble a snapshot, whereas a long poem is cinematic in nature, more closely related to film. For myself, I find it more helpful to think of poetry as radiophonic. Poetry, like radio, enjoys the open space that surrounds it, and invites the imagination to fill that space. On the radio, that space is silence and the absence of any visual stimulation; in poetry, that space is empty white paper surrounding the text. In a short poem, a whole universe can be concocted in just a couple of lines, with an emotional pull – like a gravitational force drawing the reader towards its core. The short poem is poetry taken at its word. If it is the absolute right of poetry to fall short of the right hand margin, then it is the same right that allows a poem to pull up before the bottom of the page. And if it is in the nature of poetry to show by example, then it is the instinct of the short poem to take that principle one stage further. The metaphor of the metaphor. Concentration, in its concentrated form.

So much for the game plan; I should now say something about picking the team. In terms of how small a piece of writing has to be before it qualifies as 'short', I have taken the upper limit to be thirteen lines. This is an arbitrary figure, of course, but I see the sonnet as some kind of threshold or watershed, at which point brevity is no longer the main issue. It has been interesting in researching this collection to note how many poems do claw their way towards that magic number of fourteen, as if in reaching it a poem might suddenly be imbued with extra meaning. Using the sonnet as a yardstick ruled out a number of great poems. It also exposed certain pieces – pieces I'd always thought of as free-wheeling, spontaneous creations – as exercises in fourteen-line literary brown-nosing, numerically sucking up to the conventions of verse. Students of chronology will be aware that while the year, the month and the day are all naturally occurring phenomena, the week, as a passage of time, is a man-made invention. In those terms, the sonnet might be thought of as the poetic equivalent of the fortnight. The number thirteen might be just as meaningless, but what kind of fool would tempt fate by saying so?

The lower limit I have taken to be no lines at all, with no text except for a title to indicate that the poem does actually exist.

As for the type of short poem, I have practised a number of judgements. As far as I can tell, there are two kinds of poets: those who want to tell stories and sing songs, and those who want to work out the chemical equation for language and pass on their experiments as poems. I'm interested in both but prefer the first, and when it comes to putting together an anthology, there's no point in having a party if you can't invite your friends. I have taken the term 'poem' to mean any contained unit of words that seems to have a life beyond ordinary function. The definition of poetry is not the subject of this book, and a long time ago I settled for the argument that says a poem is a poem when its context declares it: e.g., here is a group of words that appears alongside other poems, in a book with the word poetry in its title, edited by a poet, published by a press famous for publishing poetry: it is a poem. Some of the poems included are indeed short and sweet, others are more sweet and sour, and some are of the short sharp shock variety. I considered many types of writing, including song lyrics, sacred prayers, obscene limericks, found poems, poetic fragments, even prose, but in the end settled mainly for . . . well, poems. I felt a strong obligation to include at least one haiku, and for that reason have not done so.

When reading through, I was surprised by the number of very strong pieces whose subject was death, and have come to wonder if this is because of the short poem's relationship with the epitaph. Presumably more care is taken when words are to be inscribed by a chisel, when the author has less space to work in, and when the message must summarize a person's life.

I have tried to avoid extracting poems from larger poetic surroundings, such as sequences, cycles, or poems taken from dramatic works, but poetry exists in such a complicated variety of environments that this was not always possible. I also set out with the intention of allowing no more than one poem per poet, but this would have been to put the writer above the writing – a common enough mistake without me adding to it. There is also the question of the poet's intent versus the restrictions of typographical reproduction. Robert Frost's 'A Leaf-Treader' is a twelve-line poem to my mind, but paper width and point size nearly always lead to three or four of its lines running over. It is a short poem in spirit if not in print.

The anthology is arranged as a countdown, beginning with the longest poem and finishing with the smallest. Possibly it continues beyond the end of the book towards some vanishing point in the distance.

SHORT AND SWEET

'After great pain, a formal feeling comes'

After great pain, a formal feeling comes –
The Nerves sit ceremonious, like Tombs –
The stiff Heart questions was it He, that bore,
And Yesterday, or Centuries before?

The Feet, mechanical, go round –
Of Ground, or Air, or Ought –
A Wooden way
Regardless grown,
A Quartz contentment, like a stone –

This is the Hour of Lead –
Remembered, if outlived,
As Freezing persons, recollect the Snow –
First – Chill – then Stupor – then the letting go –

Success

I

I was invincibly attracted to her;
Only an abyss can exercise such fascination.

II

I paused under a locust-tree, lighting a cigarette:
The water has our mark on it still.

III

She told me at night, the time of living breath;
We took a shower in perfect darkness.

IV

Was that the distant roar of lions
Or the sounds of the clouds travelling?

V

When a pregnant woman bows to a fertile idol
The unborn child bows as she does, within the
     temple.

VI

So I went out and walked round the lake again
To listen to the sky; approaching thunder
Printed its paw-marks across the water.

'I stood on a tower in the wet'

I stood on a tower in the wet,
And New Year and Old Year met,
And winds were roaring and blowing;
And I said, 'O years, that meet in tears,
Have ye aught that is worth the knowing?
Science enough and exploring,
Wanderers coming and going,
Matter enough for deploring,
But aught that is worth the knowing?'
Seas at my feet were flowing,
Waves on the shingle pouring,
Old Year roaring and blowing,
And New Year blowing and roaring.

As He Found Her

She lay a long time as he found her,
Half on her side, askew, her cheek pressed to the floor.
He sat at the table there and watched,
His mind sometimes all over the place,
And then asking over and over
If she were dead: 'Are you dead, Poll, are you dead?'

For these hours, each one dressed in its figure
On the mantelpiece, love sits with him.
Habit, mutuality, sweetheartedness,
Drop through his body,
And he is not able now to touch her –
A bar of daylight, no more than
Across a table, flows between them.

He Resigns

Age, and the deaths, and the ghosts.
Her having gone away
in spirit from me. Hosts
of regrets come & find me empty.

I don't feel this will change.
I don't want any thing
or person, familiar or strange.
I don't think I will sing

any more just now,
or ever. I must start
to sit with a blind brow
above an empty heart.

Late Air

From a magician's midnight sleeve
  the radio-singers
distribute all their love-songs
over the dew-wet lawns.
  And like a fortune-teller's
their marrow-piercing guesses are whatever
   you believe.

But on the Navy Yard aerial I find
  better witnesses
for love on summer nights.
Five remote red lights
  keep their nests there; Phoenixes
burning quietly, where the dew cannot climb.

WILLIAM BLAKE

The Garden of Love

I went to the Garden of Love,
And saw what I never had seen:
A Chapel was built in the midst,
Where I used to play on the green.

And the gates of this Chapel were shut,
And 'Thou shalt not' writ over the door;
So I turn'd to the Garden of Love
That so many sweet flowers bore;

And I saw it was filled with graves,
And tomb-stones where flowers should be;
And Priests in black gowns were walking their
    rounds,
And binding with briars my joys & desires.

To My Dear and Loving Husband

If ever two were one, then surely we.
If ever man were loved by wife, then thee;
If ever wife was happy in a man,
Compare with me, ye women, if you can.
I prize thy love more than whole mines of gold,
Or all the riches that the East doth hold.
My love is such that rivers cannot quench,
Nor aught but love from thee give recompense.
Thy love is such I can no way repay;
The heavens reward thee manifold, I pray.
Then while we live, in love let's so persever,
That when we live no more we may live ever.

Spellbound

The night is darkening round me,
The wild winds coldly blow;
But a tyrant spell has bound me
And I cannot, cannot go.

The giant trees are bending
Their bare boughs weighed with snow.
And the storm is fast descending,
And yet I cannot go.

Clouds beyond clouds above me,
Wastes beyond wastes below;
But nothing drear can move me;
I will not, cannot go.

'So, we'll go no more a roving'

So, we'll go no more a-roving
   So late into the night,
Though the heart be still as loving,
   And the moon be still as bright.

For the sword outwears its sheath,
   And the soul wears out the breast,
And the heart must pause to breathe,
   And love itself have rest.

Though the night was made for loving,
   And the day returns too soon,
Yet we'll go no more a-roving
   By the light of the moon.

Second Marriage

The sky stops crying and in a sudden smile
Of childish sunshine the rain steams on the roofs;
Widow who has married widower
Poses outside the Registry for photographs.

Their grown up children are there
And damp confetti like a burst from a bag
Accumulated from a morning's marriages
Is second-hand for them against the door.

In the wood of the world where neither of them is lost
They take each other by the hand politely;
Borrowers going to and from the Library
Pass through the group as if it were a ghost.

Flowers

Some men never think of it.
You did. You'd come along
And say you'd nearly brought me flowers
But something had gone wrong.

The shop was closed. Or you had doubts –
The sort that minds like ours
Dream up incessantly. You thought
I might not want your flowers.

It made me smile and hug you then.
Now I can only smile.
But, look, the flowers you nearly brought
Have lasted all this while.

love this!

From the Irish

According to Dineen, a Gael unsurpassed
in lexicographical enterprise, the Irish
for moon means 'the white circle in a slice
of half-boiled potato or turnip'. A star
is the mark on the forehead of a beast
and the sun is the bottom of a lake, or well.

Well, if I say to you your face
is like a slice of half-boiled turnip,
your hair is the colour of a lake's bottom
and at the centre of each of your eyes
is the mark of the beast, it is because
I want to love you properly, according to Dineen.

The Ideal

This is where I came from.
I passed this way.
This should not be shameful
Or hard to say.

A self is a self.
It is not a screen.
A person should respect
What he has been.

This is my past
Which I shall not discard.
This is the ideal.
This is hard.

A Leaf-Treader

I have been treading on leaves all day until I am
    autumn-tired.
God knows all the colour and form of leaves I have
    trodden on and mired.
Perhaps I have put forth too much strength and been
    too fierce from fear.
I have safely trodden underfoot the leaves of another
    year.

All summer long they were overhead, more lifted up
    than I.
To come to their final place in earth they had to pass
    me by.
All summer long I thought I heard them threatening
    under their breath.
And when they came it seemed with a will to carry
    me with them to death.

They spoke to the fugitive in my heart as if it were
    leaf to leaf.
They tapped at my eyelids and touched my lips with
    an invitation to grief.
But it was no reason I had to go because they had
    to go.
Now up my knee to keep on top of another year
    of snow.

The Stepping Stones

I have my yellow boots on to walk
Across the shires where I hide
Away from my true people and all
I can't put easily into my life.

So you will see I am stepping on
The stones between the runnels getting
Nowhere nowhere. It is almost
Embarrassing to be alive alone.

Take my hand and pull me over from
The last stone on to the moss and
The three celandines. Now my dear
Let us go home across the shires.

The Announcement

They came, the brothers, and took two chairs
    In their usual quiet way;
And for a time we did not think
    They had much to say.

And they began and talked awhile
    Of ordinary things,
Till spread that silence in the room
    A pent thought brings.

And then they said: 'The end has come.
    Yes: it has come at last.'
And we looked down, and knew that day
    A spirit had passed.

My First Bra

A big brown bear
is knocking at the door:

he wants to borrow a dress
and matching knickers.

The smell of lilac
smothers me like wool;

beyond the lawns,
I hear my naked sister

crying in the nettles
where I threw her:

*nobody else is having
my first bra.*

'Loveliest of trees, the cherry now'

Loveliest of trees, the cherry now
Is hung with bloom along the bough,
And stands about the woodland ride
Wearing white for Eastertide.

Now, of my threescore years and ten,
Twenty will not come again,
And take from seventy springs a score,
It only leaves me fifty more.

And since to look at things in bloom
Fifty springs are little room,
Above the woodlands I will go
To see the cherry hung with snow.

The Diamond Cutter

Not what the light will do but how he shapes it
And what particular colours it will bear,

And something of the climber's concentration
Seeing the white peak, setting the right foot there.

Not how the sun was plausible at morning
Nor how it was distributed at noon,

And not how much the single stone could show
But rather how much brilliance it would shun;

Simply a paring down, a cleaving to
One object, as the star-gazer who sees

One single comet polished by its fall
Rather than countless, untouched galaxies.

The Base

Poison is in the wood. The sap
Runs thin, the bark sheds off. We scaled
The tallest pine and found it rotting at the top.

And yet the lower leaves are green,
Or almost green, and scarcely thinning
Where the light is kind. Who sealed

Those veins and faked that color could
Shrivel the world's enormous skin
And make it burn and glow

Like all the lights of Europe. So
It burns and burns. The sap runs thin.
And here we build, and gather, and are fed.

The Winter Palace

Most people know more as they get older:
I give all that the cold shoulder.

I spent my second quarter-century
Losing what I had learnt at university

And refusing to take in what had happened since.
Now I know none of the names in the public prints,

And am starting to give offence by forgetting faces
And swearing I've never been in certain places.

It will be worth it, if in the end I manage
To blank out whatever it is that is doing the damage.

Then there will be nothing I know.
My mind will fold into itself, like fields, like snow.

D. H. LAWRENCE

Piano

Softly, in the dusk, a woman is singing to me;
Taking me back down the vista of years, till I see
A child sitting under the piano, in the boom of the
　　tingling strings
And pressing the small, poised feet of a mother
　　who smiles as she sings.

In spite of myself, the insidious mastery of song
Betrays me back, till the heart of me weeps to belong
To the old Sunday evenings at home, with winter
　　outside
And hymns in the cosy parlour, the tinkling piano
　　our guide.

So now it is vain for the singer to burst into clamour
With the great black piano appassionato. The
　　glamour
Of childish days is upon me, my manhood is cast
Down in the flood of remembrance, I weep like a child
　　for the past.

Animals

Have you forgotten what we were like then
when we were still first rate
and the day came fat with an apple in its mouth

it's no use worrying about Time
but we did have a few tricks up our sleeves
and turned some sharp corners

the whole pasture looked like our meal
we didn't need speedometers
we could manage cocktails out of ice and water

I wouldn't want to be faster
or greener than now if you were with me O you
were the best of all my days

Sinking

O I am spent, I have no more strength to swim.
The blessed sun touches the bitter sea's rim:
I cannot see the headland or the little town,
All my limbs are weary, and I must go down.

O is it sleep or love or death I most need,
And what peace shall I find in the arms of the weed?
The gulf-weed shall take me and cradle me in brown
Wide-waving tresses, for I must go down.

Go down under the sweet, the bitter flow:
You are the blind, but the blessed spirits know
Whether in sleep, or love, or death you must drown;
Cease then your striving, sink and go down.

CHRISTOPHER REID

Fetish

I have in my possession
an angel's wingbone:
valueless, I gather,
without the certificate
of authentication
which can only be signed by a bishop.

I treasure it, however,
and almost religiously love
the sweet feel of its curve
between thumb and forefinger
deep in my jacket pocket,
the way I'm fondling it now.

Oyster

Bandage your hand
against the bladed shell,
work the knife well into the slot
(imagine a paint-scraper at a rusted rim)
and prise the lid off,
keeping the juices in.

Raise carefully to the chin
then bite the tongue out by the root;
suck it from its mouth of pearl
and chew, never swallow.
This is not sex, remember:
you are eating the sea.

Coming to This

We have done what we wanted.
We have discarded dreams, preferring the heavy
    industry
of each other, and we have welcomed grief
and called ruin the impossible habit to break.

And now we are here.
The dinner is ready and we cannot eat.
The meat sits in the white lake of its dish.
The wine waits.

Coming to this
has its rewards: nothing is promised, nothing is
    taken away.
We have no heart or saving grace,
no place to go, no reason to remain.

Bodybuilders' Contest

From scalp to sole, all muscles in slow motion.
The ocean of his torso drips with lotion.
The king of all is he who preens and wrestles
with sinews twisted into monstrous pretzels.

Onstage, he grapples with a grizzly bear
the deadlier for not really being there.
Three unseen panthers are in turn laid low,
each with one smoothly choreographed blow.

He grunts while showing his poses and paces.
His back alone has twenty different faces.
The mammoth fist he raises as he wins
is tribute to the force of vitamins.

On a Wedding Anniversary

The sky is torn across
This ragged anniversary of two
Who moved for three years in tune
Down the long walks of their vows.

Now their love lies a loss
And Love and his patients roar on a chain;
From every true or crater
Carrying cloud, Death strikes their house.

Too late in the wrong rain
They come together whom their love parted:
The windows pour into their heart
And the doors burn in their brain.

WILLIAM CARLOS WILLIAMS

This is Just to Say

I have eaten
the plums
that were in
the icebox

and which
you were probably
saving
for breakfast

Forgive me
they were delicious
so sweet
and so cold

The Lake Isle of Innisfree

I will arise and go now, and go to Innisfree,
And a small cabin build there, of clay and wattles
    made:
Nine bean-rows will I have there, a hive for the
    honey-bee,
And live alone in the bee-loud glade.

And I shall have some peace there, for peace
    comes dropping slow,
Dropping from the veils of the morning to where
    the cricket sings;
There midnight's all a glimmer, and noon a
    purple glow,
And evening full of the linnet's wings.

I will arise and go now, for always night and day
I hear lake water lapping with low sounds by the
    shore;
While I stand on the roadway, or on the pavements
    grey,
I hear it in the deep heart's core.

The Knight's Tomb

Where is the grave of Sir Arthur O'Kellyn?
Where may the grave of that good man be? –
By the side of a spring, on the breast of Helvellyn,
Under the twigs of a young birch tree!
The oak that in summer was sweet to hear,
And rustled its leaves in the fall of the year,
And whistled and roared in the winter alone,
Is gone, – and the birch in its stead is grown. –
The Knight's bones are dust,
And his good sword rust; –
His soul is with the saints, I trust.

Pied Beauty

Glory be to God for dappled things –
   For skies of couple-colour as a brinded cow;
      For rose-moles all in stipple upon trout that swim;
Fresh-firecoal chestnut-falls; finches' wings;
   Landscape plotted and pieced – fold, fallow,
      and plough;
      And áll trádes, their gear and tackle and trim.
All things counter, original, spare, strange;
   Whatever is fickle, freckled (who knows how?)
      With swift, slow; sweet, sour; adazzle, dim;
He fathers-forth whose beauty is past change:
      Praise him.

IAN MCMILLAN

The Prince of Wales Visits Alnwick

(from a photograph)

The prince is a blur in his fast car.
A hand waves from a thin crowd.

There is a man in knickerbockers.
There are two women leaning from windows.

There are two men at the cobbler's door.
There is a mend up the middle

where the photograph has been torn.
There is a single word behind the head

of the speeding prince: Simpson,
a shop-sign in the grey background

like a bullet with his name on it.

'Gently dip, but not too deep'

Gently dip, but not too deep,
For fear you make the golden beard to weep.
Fair maiden, white and red,
Comb me smooth, and stroke my head;
And thou shalt have some cockle bread.

Gently dip, but not too deep,
For fear thou make the golden beard to weep.
Fair maiden, white and red,
Comb me smooth, and stroke my head;
And every hair a sheave shall be,
And every sheave a golden tree.

Sleeping at Last

Sleeping at last, the trouble and tumult over,
  Sleeping at last, the struggle and horror past,
Cold and white, out of sight of friend and of lover,
      Sleeping at last.

  No more a tired heart downcast or overcast,
No more pangs that wring or shifting fears that
      hover,
  Sleeping at last in a dreamless sleep locked fast.

Fast asleep. Singing birds in their leafy cover
  Cannot wake her, nor shake her the gusty blast.
Under the purple thyme and the purple clover
      Sleeping at last.

'In the desert'

In the desert
I saw a creature, naked, bestial,
Who, squatting upon the ground,
Held his heart in his hands,
And ate of it.
I said, 'Is it good, friend?'
'It is bitter – bitter,' he answered;
'But I like it
Because it is bitter,
And because it is my heart.'

'in spite of everything'

in spite of everything
which breathes and moves,since Doom
(with white longest hands
neatening each crease)
will smooth entirely our minds

– before leaving my room
i turn,and(stooping
through the morning)kiss
this pillow,dear
where our heads lived and were.

Catch

There once was a fisherman of Scrabster
Caught in his pot a gey queer lapster.

Thought he, this lapster's a sure sellar,
A tail it has, and a wee propellor,

In fact, it's no ordinary lapster felly,
It looks far more like a peedie heli –

You know yon kind of hoverlapster,
A what do you call it, helicapster.

Aye, aye, it's a peedie helicapster:
There's lots are caught in the sea off Scrabster.

Public Bar TV

On a flaked ridge of the desert

Outriders have found foul water. They say nothing;
With the cactus and the petrified tree
Crouch numbed by a wind howling all
Visible horizons equally empty.

The wind brings dust and nothing
Of the wives, the children, the grandmothers
With the ancestral bones, who months ago
Left the last river,

Coming at the pace of oxen.

I Had a Dove

I had a dove and the sweet dove died;
   And I have thought it died of grieving:
O, what could it grieve for? Its feet were tied,
   With a silken thread of my own hand's weaving;
   Sweet little red feet! why should you die –
Why should you leave me, sweet bird! Why?
You lived alone in the forest-tree,
Why, pretty thing! would you not live with me?
I kissed you oft and gave you white peas;
Why not live sweetly, as in the green trees?

The Fishing Party

Because he loves off-duty policemen and their
    murderers
Christ is still seen walking on the water of Lough
    Neagh,
Whose fingers created bluebottles, meadow-
    browns, red
Admirals, painted ladies, fire-flies, and are tying
    now
Woodcock hackles around hooks, lamb's wool,
    badger fur

Until about his head swarm artificial flies and their
    names,
Dark Mackerel, Gravel Bed, Greenwell's Glory,
    Soldier
Palmer, Coachman, Water Cricket, Orange Grouse,
    Barm,
Without snagging in his hair or ceasing to circle
    above
Policemen turned by gunmen into fishermen for
    ever.

Canon

Beside the paper-mill at Burneside, Westmorland

I only spoke to see the tree
In flood – I only spoke to see.

I only looked to hear the weir
In song – I only looked to hear.

I listened just to tell the yel-
low rag – I listened just to tell

The yellow ragtail how to show
And teach the yellow ragwort how

I only came for speech of beech
And beck – I only came for speech.

Example

A butterfly flew between the cars.
Marie José said: it must be Chuang Tzu,
on a tour of New York.
                              But the butterfly
didn't know it was a butterfly
dreaming it was Chuang Tzu
                                        or Chuang Tzu
dreaming he was a butterfly.
The butterfly never wondered:
                                        it flew.

Translated by Eliot Weinberger

Everyone Sang

Everyone suddenly burst out singing;
And I was filled with such delight
As prisoned birds must find in freedom,
Winging wildly across the white
Orchards and dark-green fields; on – on – and out
   of sight.

Everyone's voice was suddenly lifted;
And beauty came like the setting sun:
My heart was shaken with tears; and horror
Drifted away . . . O, but Everyone
Was a bird; and the song was wordless; the singing
   will never be done.

Five Years Old

Stars fell all night.
The iceman had been very generous that day
with his chips and slivers.

And I buried my pouch of jewels
inside a stone casket under the porch,
their beauty saved for another world.

And then my sister came home
and I threw a dart through her cheek
and cried all night,

so much did I worship her.

CHARLES CAUSLEY

I Am the Song

I am the song that sings the bird.
I am the leaf that grows the land.
I am the tide that moves the moon.
I am the stream that halts the sand.
I am the cloud that drives the storm.
I am the earth that lights the sun.
I am the fire that strikes the stone.
I am the clay that shapes the hand.
I am the word that speaks the man.

Fire and Ice

Some say the world will end in fire,
Some say in ice.
From what I've tasted of desire
I hold with those who favor fire.
But if it had to perish twice,
I think I know enough of hate
To say that for destruction ice
Is also great
And would suffice.

The Brandy Glass

Only let it form within his hands once more –
The moment cradled like a brandy glass.
Sitting alone in the empty dining hall . . .
From the chandeliers the snow begins to fall
Piling around carafes and table legs
And chokes the passage of the revolving door.
The last diner, like a ventriloquist's doll
Left by his master, gazes before him, begs:
'Only let it form within my hands once more.'

Captain Lavender

Night-hours. The edge of a fuller moon
waits among the interlocking patterns
of a flier's sky.

Sperm names, ovum names, push inside
each other. We are half-taught
our real names, from other lives.

Emphasise your eyes. Be my flare-
path, my uncold begetter,
my air-minded bird-sense.

To Whom It May Concern

This poem about ice cream
has nothing to do with government,
with riot, with any political scheme.

It is a poem about ice cream. You see?
About how you might stroll into a shop
and ask: *One Strawberry Split. One Mivvi.*

What did I tell you? No one will die.
No licking tongues will melt like candle wax.
This is a poem about ice cream. Do not cry.

Pad, pad

I always remember your beautiful flowers
And the beautiful kimono you wore
When you sat on the couch
With that tigerish crouch
And told me you loved me no more.

What I cannot remember is how I felt when
    you were unkind
All I know is, if you were unkind now I should
    not mind.
Ah me, the power to feel exaggerated, angry and sad
The years have taken from me. Softly I go now, pad
    pad.

The Rainbow

My heart leaps up when I behold
   A rainbow in the sky:
So was it when my life began,
So is it now I am a man,
So be it when I shall grow old,
   Or let me die!
The child is father of the man;
And I could wish my days to be
Bound each to each by natural piety.

'I have been a foster long and many day'

I have been a foster long and many day;
    My lockès been hore.
I shall hang up my horn by the grene wode spray;
    Foster will I be no more.

All the whiles that I may my bowe bende
    Shall I weddè no wife.
I shall bigge me a bowr at the wodès ende,
    There to lede my life.

foster: forester

Gare du Midi

A nondescript express in from the South,
Crowds round the ticket barrier, a face
To welcome which the mayor has not contrived
Bugles or braid: something about the mouth
Distracts the stray look with alarm and pity.
Snow is falling. Clutching a little case,
He walks out briskly to infect a city
Whose terrible future may have just arrived.

Taxman

Seven scythes leaned at the wall.
Beard upon golden beard
The last barley load
Swayed through the yard.
The girls uncorked the ale.
Fiddle and feet moved together.
Then between stubble and heather
A horseman rode.

'Of all our bath-house thieves the cleverest one'

Of all our bath-house thieves the cleverest one
Is you, Vibennius, with your pansy son.
(The old man's fingers suffer from a heinous
Itch, but the boy's as grasping with his anus.)
Why not deport yourselves, go anywhere
The weather's horrible? For all Rome's aware
Of Father's pilferings, and believe me, Sonny,
That hairy rump won't make you any money.

Translated by James Michie

On Roofs of Terry Street

Television aerials, Chinese characters
In the lower sky, wave gently in the smoke.

Nest-building sparrows peck at moss,
Urban flora and fauna, soft, unscrupulous.

Rain drying on the slates shines sometimes.
A builder is repairing someone's leaking roof,

He kneels upright to rest his back,
His trowel catches the light and becomes precious.

[From the Sleeping House]

Look down from a height on the long
Oystercatching shore of Loch
Long at first light with the tide
Streaming out between the pools
And you will see. Don't breathe
Or frighten me waiting to meet
My dear from the sleeping house coming
Over the shingle with her bare feet.

Heaven-Haven

A nun takes the veil

I have desired to go
   Where springs not fail,
To fields where flies no sharp and sided hail
   And a few lilies blow.

And I have asked to be
   Where no storms come,
Where the green swell is in the havens dumb,
   And out of the swing of the sea.

A Jelly-Fish

Visible, invisible,
   A fluctuating charm
an amber-tinctured amethyst
   inhabits it, your arm
approaches and it opens
   and it closes; you had meant
to catch it and it quivers;
   you abandon your intent.

Bog-Face

Dear little Bog-Face,
Why are you so cold?
And why do you lie with your eyes shut? –
You are not very old.

I am a Child of this World,
And a Child of Grace,
And Mother, I shall be glad when it is over,
I am Bog-Face.

Weather Report

Light wind at Grand Prairie, drifting snow.
Low at Vermilion, forty degrees of frost.
Lost in the Barrens, hunting over spines of ice,
the great sled dog Shadow is running for his life.

All who hear – in your wide horizon of thought
caught in this cold, the world all going gray –
pray for the frozen dead at Yellow Knife.
These words we send are becoming parts of their night.

Snow

In the gloom of whiteness,
In the great silence of snow,
A child was sighing
And bitterly saying: 'Oh,
They have killed a white bird up there on her nest,
The down is fluttering from her breast!'
And still it fell through that dusky brightness
On the child crying for the bird of the snow.

When I Heard the Learn'd Astronomer

When I heard the learn'd astronomer,
When the proofs, the figures, were ranged in
    columns before me,
When I was shown the charts and diagrams, to
    add, divide, and measure them,
When I sitting heard the astronomer where he
    lectured with much applause in the lecture-room,
How soon unaccountable I became tired and sick,
Till rising and gliding out I wander'd off by myself,
In the mystical moist night-air, and from time to
    time,
Look'd up in perfect silence at the stars.

'The enemy of life'

The enemy of life, decayer of all kind,
That with his cold withers away the green,
This other night me in my bed did find,
And offered me to rid my fever clean;
And I did grant, so did despair me blind.
He drew his bow with arrow sharp and keen,
And struck the place where love had hit before,
And drove the first dart deeper more and more.

Lust

Lust is at home here and I make it welcome.
I offer it stuff it accepts but would otherwise take.
    Beautiful telling ache.
Lust will be last to leave this all-nite affair,
    Make no mistake,
    And it was welcome,
    But I live here.

W. H. AUDEN

Epitaph on a Tyrant

Perfection, of a kind, was what he was after,
And the poetry he invented was easy to understand;
He knew human folly like the back of his hand,
And was greatly interested in armies and fleets;
When he laughed, respectable senators burst with
    laughter,
And when he cried the little children died in the
    streets.

Epitaph for the Poet

The single sleeper lying here
    Is neither lying nor asleep.
Bend down your nosey parker ear
    And eavesdrop on him. In the deep
Conundrum of the dirt he speaks
    The one word you will never hear.

A Burnt Ship

Out of a fired ship, which, by no way
But drowning, could be rescued from the flame,
Some men leap'd forth, and ever as they came
Near the foes' ships, did by their shot decay;
So all were lost, which in the ship were found,
   They in the sea being burnt, they in the burnt
     ship drown'd.

The Hanging Man

By the roots of my hair some god got hold of me.
I sizzled in his blue volts like a desert prophet.

The nights snapped out of sight like a lizard's eyelid:
A world of bald white days in a shadeless socket.

A vulturous boredom pinned me in this tree.
If he were I, he would do what I did.

Goodtime Jesus

Jesus got up one day a little later than usual. He had been dreaming so deep there was nothing left in his head. What was it? A nightmare, dead bodies walking all around him, eyes rolled back, skin falling off. But he wasn't afraid of that. It was a beautiful day. How 'bout some coffee? Don't mind if I do. Take a little ride on my donkey, I love that donkey. Hell, I love everybody.

'Foweles in the frith'

Foweles in the frith,
The fisses in the flod,
And I mon waxe wod:
Mulch sorw I walke with
For beste of bon and blod.

frith: wood; *flod*: river; *waxe wod*: go mad

Mrs Darwin

7 April 1852.
Went to the Zoo.
I said to Him –
Something about that Chimpanzee over there
    reminds me of you.

RANDALL JARRELL

The Death of the Ball Turret Gunner

From my mother's sleep I fell into the State,
And I hunched in its belly till my wet fur froze.
Six miles from earth, loosed from its dream of life,
I woke to black flak and the nightmare fighters.
When I died they washed me out of the turret with a
  hose.

Ireland

The Volkswagen parked in the gap,
But gently ticking over.
You wonder if it's lovers
And not men hurrying back
Across two fields and a river.

'Westron wind, when will thou blow'

Westron wind, when will thou blow,
The small rain down can rain?
Christ if my love were in my arms,
And I in my bed again.

The Lion

O lion, mournful image
Of kings sadly brought down,
You are born now only in cages
In Hamburg, among the Germans.

An Expedition

Down to the end of the garden in the night.
With cigarette and glass of ice-cold milk.
I pick my way over heaps of builders' rubble.
Light from the new kitchen window comes along too.

Epitaph on an Unfortunate Artist

He found a formula for drawing comic rabbits:
This formula for drawing comic rabbits paid,
So in the end he could not change the tragic habits
This formula for drawing comic rabbits made.

Love Without Hope

Love without hope, as when the young bird-catcher
Swept off his tall hat to the Squire's own daughter,
So let the imprisoned larks escape and fly
Singing about her head, as she rode by.

TONY HARRISON

The Bedbug

Comrade, with your finger on the playback switch,
Listen carefully to each love-moan,
And enter in the file which cry is real, and which
A mere performance for your microphone.

The Rescue

In drifts of sleep I came upon you
Buried to your waist in snow.
You reached your arms out: I came to
Like water in a dream of thaw.

I Had Hope When Violence Was Ceas't

Dawnlight freezes against the east-wire.
The guards cough 'raus! 'raus! We flinch and grin,
Our flesh oozing towards its last outrage.
That which is taken from me is not mine.

Epilogue

I have crossed an ocean
I have lost my tongue
from the root of the old one
a new one has sprung

The Bath Tub

As a bathtub lined with white porcelain,
When the hot water gives out or goes tepid,
So is the slow cooling of our chivalrous passion,
O my much praised but-not-altogether-satisfactory
   lady.

TOMAŽ ŠALAMUN

[untitled]

White,
older brother of a wedding guest,
don't wait for mist,
don't wait for rice.

Translated by the author and Michael Waltuch

ANNE STEVENSON

The Mother

Of course I love them, they are my children.
That is my daughter and this my son.
And this is my life I give them to please them.
It has never been used. Keep it safe. Pass it on.

Lights Out

We're allowed to talk for ten minutes
about what has happened during the day,
then we have to go to sleep.
It doesn't matter what we dream about.

DAVID CONSTANTINE

Coltsfoot

Coming before my birthday they are forever your
 flowers
Who are dead and at whose hand
I picked them on the allotments and blitzed land.

'An Hour is a Sea'

An Hour is a Sea
Between a few, and me –
With them would Harbor be –

TOMAŽ ŠALAMUN

[untitled]

Who's better,
a god with a beard or a god without a beard?
A god with a beard.

Translated by the author and Elliot Anderson

W. B. YEATS

Three Movements

Shakespearean fish swam the sea, far away from land;
Romantic fish swam in nets coming to the hand;
What are all those fish that lie gasping on the strand?

CHRISTOPHER LOGUE

To a Friend in Search of Rural Seclusion

When all else fails,
Try Wales.

'Night crept up on them'

Night crept up on them

                black sleep closed their eyes

Evening Chess

The Black Queen raised high
In my father's angry hand.

GAVIN EWART

Penal

The clanking and wanking of Her Majesty's prisons.

EDWIN MORGAN

Siesta of a Hungarian Snake

s   sz   sz   SZ   sz   SZ   sz   ZS   zs   ZS   zs   zs   z

Found

These sleeping tablets may cause drowsiness.

DON PATERSON

On Going to Meet a Zen Master in the Kyushu Mountains and Not Finding Him

for A.G.

ACKNOWLEDGEMENTS

The editor and publishers gratefully acknowledge permission to reprint copyright material in this book as follows:

W. H. AUDEN: Faber and Faber Ltd for 'Gare du Midi' and 'Epigraph on a Tyrant' from *Collected Poems* (1994); GEORGE BARKER: Faber and Faber Ltd for 'Epitaph for the Poet' from *Collected Poems* (1987); JOHN BERRYMAN: Faber and Faber Ltd for 'He Resigns' from *Collected Poems* (1990); ELIZABETH BISHOP 'Late Air' from *The Complete Poems 1927–1979* by Elizabeth Bishop, copyright © 1979, 1983 by Alice Helen Methfessel, reprinted by permission of Farrar, Straus & Giroux, Inc.; CHARLES CAUSLEY: David Higham Associates for 'I am the Song' from *Collected Poems* (Macmillan); DAVID CONSTANTINE: Bloodaxe Books for 'Coltsfoot' from *Selected Poems* (1991); WENDY COPE: Faber and Faber Ltd for 'Flowers' from *Serious Concerns* (1992); E. E. CUMMINGS: 'in spite of everything' from *Complete Poems 1904–1962*, by E. E. Cummings, edited by George J. Firmage, by permission of W. W. Norton & Company, copyright © 1991 by the Trustees for the E. E. Cummings Trust and George James Firmage; EMILY DICKINSON: poems 341 and 825, reprinted by permission of the publishers and the Trustees of Amherst College from *The Poems of Emily Dickinson*, Thomas H. Johnson, ed., Cambridge, Mass.: the Belknap Press of Harvard University Press, copyright © 1951, 1955, 1979, 1983 by the President and Fellows of Harvard College; PETER DIDSBURY: Bloodaxe Books for 'An Expedition' from *That Old-Time Religion* (1994); DOUGLAS DUNN: Faber and Faber Ltd for 'On the Roofs of Terry Street' from *Selected Poems* (1986); JAMES FENTION: Peters Fraser & Dunlop Group Ltd for 'The Ideal' from *Out of Danger* (Penguin); W. S. GRAHAM: '[From the Sleeping House]' and 'The Stepping Stones' from *Selected Poems* (Faber, 1996), by kind permission of Margaret Snow on behalf of Nessie Graham; ROBERT GRAVES: Carcanet Press Limited for 'Epitaph on an Unfortunate Artist' and 'Love Without Hope' from *Collected Poems* (1986); TONY HARRISON: Gordon Dickerson on behalf of the author for 'The Bed Bug' from *Selected Poems* (Penguin, 1984); SEAMUS HEANEY: Faber and Faber Ltd for 'The Rescue' from *Opened Ground: Poems 1966–1996* (1998); SELIMA HILL: Bloodaxe Books for 'My First Bra' from *Trembling Hearts in the Bodies of Dogs: New and Selected Poems*

(1994); TED HUGHES: Faber and Faber Ltd for 'Public Bar TV' from *New Selected Poems 1957–1994* (1995); RANDALL JARRELL: Faber and Faber Ltd for 'The Death of the Ball Turret Gunner' from *Complete Poems* (1971); ELIZABETH JENNINGS: David Higham Associates for 'The Diamond Cutter' from *Collected Poems* (Carcanet Press); WELDON KEES: Faber and Faber Ltd for 'The Base' from *Selected Poems* (1993); PHILIP LARKIN: Faber and Faber Ltd for 'The Winter Palace' from *Collected Poems* (1988); D. H. LAWRENCE: Laurence Pollinger Limited and the Estate of Frieda Lawrence Ravagli for 'Piano' from *The Complete Poems of D. H. Lawrence* (Penguin Books); CHRISTOPHER LOGUE: Faber and Faber Ltd for 'To a Friend in Search of Rural Seclusion' from *Selected Poems* (1996); LOUIS MACNEICE: David Higham Associates for 'The Brandy Glass' from *Selected Poems* (Faber, 1966); MEDBH MCGUCKIAN: 'Captain Lavender' from *Captain Lavender* (1994), by kind permission of the author and The Gallery Press; IAN MCMILLAN: Carcanet Press Ltd for 'The Prince of Wales Visits Alnwick' from *Selected Poems*; GEORGE MACKAY BROWN: John Murray for 'Taxman' from *Selected Poems*; GLYN MAXWELL: Bloodaxe Books for 'Lust' from *Rest for the Wicked* (1995); MARIANNE MOORE: Faber and Faber Ltd for 'A Jelly-Fish' from *Complete Poems* (1984); EDWIN MORGAN: Carcanet Press Ltd for 'Siesta of a Hungarian Snake' from *Selected Poems*; ANDREW MOTION: Faber and Faber Ltd for 'To Whom It May Concern' from *Selected Poems* (1998); PAUL MULDOON: Faber and Faber Ltd for 'Ireland' from *New Selected Poems* (1996); GRACE NICHOLS: Curtis Brown Group Ltd for 'Epilogue' from *The Fat Black Woman's Poems* (Virago, 1984); NORMAN NICHOLSON: Faber and Faber Ltd for 'Canon' from *Collected Poems* (1994); DON PATERSON: Faber and Faber Ltd for 'On Going to Meet...' from *God's Gift to Women* (1997); OCTAVIO PAZ: Carcanet Press Ltd for 'Example' from *Collected Poems*; RUTH PITTER: Enitharmon Press for 'Sinking' from *Collected Poems* (1996); SYLVIA PLATH: Faber and Faber Ltd for 'The Hanging Man' from *Collected Poems* (1981); EZRA POUND: Faber and Faber Ltd for 'The Bath Tub' from *Selected Poems* (1981); CHRISTOPHER REID: Faber and Faber Ltd for 'Fetish' from *Expanded Universes* (1996); SIEGFRIED SASSOON: Barbara Levy Literary Agency for 'Everyone Sang' from *The War Poems* (Faber, 1983), copyright Siegfried Sassoon, by kind permission of George Sassoon; CHARLES SIMIC: Faber and Faber Ltd for 'Evening Chess' from *Frightening Toys* (1995); STEVIE SMITH: James MacGibbon for 'Pad, pad' and 'Bog-Face' from *The Collected Poems of Stevie Smith* (Penguin Twentieth Century Classics); MARK STRAND: Carcanet

Press Ltd for 'Coming to This' from *Selected Poems*; WISŁAWA SZYMBORSKA: Faber and Faber Ltd for 'Bodybuilders' from *View with a Grain of Sand* (1996); JAMES TATE: Carcanet Press Ltd for 'Five Years Old' and 'Goodtime Jesus' from *Selected Poems*; DYLAN THOMAS: David Higham Associates for 'On a Wedding Anniversary' from *Collected Poems*; JEFFREY WAINWRIGHT: Carcanet Press Ltd for 'As He Found Her' from *Selected Poems*; HUGO WILLIAMS: Faber and Faber Ltd for 'Lights Out' from *Dock Leaves* (1994); WILLIAM CARLOS WILLIAMS: Carcanet Press Ltd for 'This is just to say' from *Collected Poems*; W. B. YEATS: 'The Lake Isle of Innisfree' from *The Collected Poems of W. B. Yeats* (Macmillan, 1985), by permisssion of A. P. Watt Ltd on behalf of Michael B. Yeats.

INDEX OF POETS

INDEX OF FIRST LINES